Waking *past* Midnight

selected poems

FLOYD COLLINS

STEPHEN F. AUSTIN STATE UNIVERSITY PRESS

Production Manager: Kimberly Verhines
Book Design: Meredith Janning
Cover Art: Alex Fu via Pexels

For more information:
Stephen F. Austin State University Press
P.O. Box 13007 SFA Station
Nacogdoches, Texas 75962
sfapress@sfasu.edu
www.sfasu.edu/sfapress
936-468-1078

Distributed by Texas A&M University Press Consortium
www.tamupress.com

ISBN: 978-1-62288-245-8

for Terry, and no other

CONTENTS

Author's Note   /   9

To Rafael Alberti   /   11
The Scarecrow   /   12
Lizard   /   13
Forecast   /   14
Piano Player   /   15
The Glassblower   /   16
Waking Past Midnight   /   17
A Last Word   /   18
Ghost of the Coal Miner   /   19
The Death of Georg Trakl (1887-1914)   /   20
The Tree House   /   22
Litany of Rain   /   23
Walk in the Cemetery at Dawn   /   24
Turning the Corner for Home   /   25
Drawing a Sea-Horse   /   26
The Priest and the Toad   /   27
Angler   /   28
Revel   /   29
A Blues Funeral Mood   /   30
Warm Latitudes   /   31
James Bowie: Bexar, 1836   /   32
The Natchez Sandbar Fight   /   34
Bonham on the Night Prairie   /   35
Travis   /   37
Alamo Pyre: March 6, 1836   /   40
Crockett   /   41
Crockett by Firelight   /   42
Gregorio Esparza   /   44
Kentucky Long Rifles   /   46
Kentucky Gunsmith: Long Rifle, 1833   /   47

Berserker / 50

Santa Anna's Spurs / 52

The Fruits of Victory / 57

Degüello / 58

Eric Von Schmidt: Beyond Canvas / 59

The Militia Shirt / 60

Aftermath: Dusk at the Alamo / 61

San Antonio De Valero / 62

Expiation / 66

Farewell / 67

The Visitation / 68

Sleeping Over on Highway 78 / 69

The Years Between / 70

The Waking Reverie / 72

The Watch / 73

The Ghostly Heart / 74

Sound Wisdom / 76

The Machinery of Night / 78

Backward Glances / 80

Narcissus to the Muse / 82

Two Parables / 87

Nighthawks / 89

Another Realm of Discourse / 91

Wavelengths / 93

Elusive Couplings / 96

Teresa: The Interlude / 98

Teresa: Nights on the Delta / 100

The Full Reckoning / 102

Acknowledgments / 105

About the Author / 107

Author's Note

I would like to thank the following individuals who made the publication of this volume of poems possible. I would like to begin with Kimberly Verhines, director of the Stephen F. Austin State University Press whose receptiveness to this project and timely advice facilitated the process at every turn. I should also commend the unselfish diligence of editorial assistants Meredith Janning and Katherine Noble, whose efforts on my behalf proved invaluable. I must also acknowledge the editors of the following literary journals—Marcus Tribbett and Janelle Collins of *The Arkansas Review*, Gerald Maa and C. J. Bartunek of *The Georgia Review*, Peter Stitt and Mark Drew of *The Gettysburg Review*, David Lynn and David Baker of *The Kenyon Review*, Ryan Wilson of *Literary Matters*, George Core of *The Sewanee Review*, R. T. Smith of *Shenandoah*, Andy Ciotola of *West Branch*, and Ralph Adamo of *The Xavier Review*. I would like to thank those individuals who endorsed the product of my labors while it lay in manuscript, in particular Keith Alexander, Sidney Burris, Joseph Candido, Cary Holladay, Kelsie Jones, Fredric Koeppel, Paula Lambert, Al Maginnes, William Page, Rebecca Steve, Michael Waters, and Richard Wooten. Special gratitude is owed to Joseph Candido and Gen Broyles for whose kindness and friendship I am indebted beyond words.

To Rafael Alberti

When the hour of your own dying approaches
like a horned owl,
who can hope to match your lament
for Fernando Villalon,
the elegy for a man buried with his watch running?

Night after night
I wear a necklace bestowed by nightmare,
beads of blue phosphor
and salt.

I know of the sea
only what you have taught me,
but I would bring you here
in this poem,
I would give you dominion
over a wave in a wheat field,
I would have you know the cry
of a whippoorwill in the branches
of a lonely birch grove
just at twilight.

Here the only angels are limestone,
lost among the marble chessmen
on the churchyard lawn.

And yet your elegies have consoled me
at the grave
of my own father,

they have let me see for myself
a dragonfly
with wings of stained-glass

nodding on this green stem
missed by the caretaker's mower.

THE SCARECROW

And sunset bestows
A cross of shadow
Upon the scarecrow.
                    Jorge Carrera Andrade

Evening lengthens a cruciform shadow.

But there is no
Crown of thorns for this tattered guardian
Of the rattling stalks.

Under a sky
Brilliant with stars
He listens for the sound of night's
Celestial clock

The slow millennium
Ticking down
In the heavy beams of the Cross.

Only children love the scarecrow,
The jagged seam
Of his smile.

Some evenings,
Just as the sun sets,
They steal into the fields.

Carefully, they unbutton his dead man's stare
And he sleeps.

LIZARD

Where the crow strops its cry
Down by the creek
This morning
I happen on a skink,
Three inches of burnished gold.
Before he's able to seep
Beneath a stone
I pinion him
At the crux of his spine.
How often he's left me
A brittle link
Of his tail,
Just enough flesh
To dampen the crow's beak.
As he writhes to get free,
Twin bands of black
Play into my fingers
Chords I never mastered
On the guitar.
His scales are no more
Than a delighted
Prickle
On a girl's
Smooth, braceleted arm.
When he bellies up in my palm,
Feigning death,
Underneath he shimmers
With pure opalescence.
Still he goes on throbbing,
A delicate vein in Salomé's throat.

FORECAST

November is the tombstone
At a wheat field's edge.

Now in the shed
Of the casket-maker

There is a harsh joy
In the hammer's rhythms

In the wheezing of an old saw. . .

It is a season
Beyond the simple
Provinces of weather

A premonition
In the golden eye of the crow.

PIANO PLAYER

When my mother died, the coffin-lid
Crooned shut, a gleam unsettled
The cat's eye. Now I savor cognac
And the lights of the boulevard,
Reach inside each key for the notes.

I remember, after the funeral,
An old bootblack at the train depot.
"Boy, I could tell you lies you wouldn't
Believe." It was late, frost splinters
Swarming, roots knuckling in the cold,

And my music scored like wormwood.
"When I was your age I had it made."
The coffin crooned, the cat's eye gleamed.
Now I chip ivory, swelter and roll;
From my vest trickles a chain of gold.

THE GLASSBLOWER

His contempt for the power
of mirrors
grows as he ages.
He remembers how,
when he was a child,
they were still held
to the mouths
of the dying.

Now on winter nights he sees
his breath rise
like smoke toward the stars,
and he knows the roads
will be locked by ice
before morning.

What little he keeps for himself
goes into cabinets.
And he has the dream
every night,
the young girl
who opens the dark veins
of her wrists
with a broken angel.

WAKING PAST MIDNIGHT

Twice in my dream
The shadow
Of a kingfisher
Crossed the dark shingles.

It was the flurry
In the aquarium
That woke me.

A Last Word

The telephone
rings like the blade of an ax
on a honing wheel.
A half-continent away
your voice shifts
the fine black gravel
in the mouthpiece:
words of stone.
Already it's twilight there.
And in a cold room,
with a brush,
you strike the last sparks
of the sun
from your hair.

GHOST OF THE COAL MINER

All night the whole mountain groans
in a single
splinter
of ancient shaft timber

and come morning
before the cock crows
the miners file
through the narrow streets of the town.

Soon the leaves will fly
and the first flakes will break
into crystal
above the spires of pine
and fir.

Again this winter the bony children
will raise
in some moonlit clearing
a snowman

its gaze black with reproach.

THE DEATH OF GEORG TRAKL (1887-1914)

Nothing beautiful about this snow
In the Ozarks, three to six inches
At most, where I listen for the hiss
Of late sled-runners after twilight

But hear only the chained tires
Of a Volvo jingling up the slow grade
One block east of the tracks.
It's 3° below zero, the coldest winter

In a half-decade. Gazing at a deer-print
Shod with ice under the full moon,
I think of the poems of Georg Trakl:
"A blue moment is purely and simply soul."

Gone forever are the quaking cemeteries
Of autumn, the purple star in a sunlit grape,
The glass of blue wine. Still I mark
In the thicket beyond the frozen creek

Bows, harps, wings, among fiery thorns.
Orion stalks a cobalt sky, and a gust
Rings this countryside with memories
Portentous as a child's mound of earth

Fallen in beneath October drizzle.
On that hill, a limestone angel, the nose
Eaten away, as if by syphilis. "O hells
Of sleep," you sang, erasing forever

Those lines of an idyllic childhood.
Your sister, "My beloved little demon,"
Who could set a snail writhing in a droplet
Of sweat as she knelt in the garden

Took a lover. And night suffered its
Transformations. In dreams, "The saint's
Flesh melted on a grill." Then came the war,
A barn with its wounded, the stench of blood

And pus and carbolic acid. You stared
Into the bore of a pistol as a child might
Peer into a keyhole. In the end you chose
Cocaine, blue and pure as Tyrolean snow.

The Tree House

I wait until well past midnight;
it wouldn't do to be seen.
It's September,
and I want a closer look at the leaves.
Perhaps I'll recognize a few next month.
Nails in wooden rungs,
surprised at the weight,
wake with the groans
of stiff rigging.
I step out onto the planks.
Dark currents of wind
move the branches
below my feet,
a child turns in his sleep:
some stranger is stealing his ship.

LITANY OF RAIN

Tonight a light rain is falling over the city,
over theater
and concert hall,
over bank and mausoleum,
over empty stadium
and park
where winged insects, brown
and jade,
turn the machinery of night.

Rain is falling over restaurants
where fire
preens itself like a fabled bird,
over oyster bars
poised on the brink of foam.
It is falling over the tenement dwellings
where a girl of twelve
pierces her ears
less out of despair
than the purest longing.

Rain glazes the walks to mirror dim barber shops
lit by tonics of blue
and amber.
It thickens the air of pawnshops
smoking with gems,
bristling with strung catgut
of violins,
gleaming with battered trumpets
and the scaly, iridescent harmonica.

Tonight, as I listen to the hum and drowse
of late traffic
in the streets below,
I wonder what further blessing I could wish
for a city I love
than this litany of rain
falling all night into the first morning of autumn.

WALK IN THE CEMETERY AT DAWN

Sometimes I think of the chisel.
Where the chisel does its work,
where the marble is gone,
there will be the empty spaces
bearing the shape of my name.
One tooth for a smile.

There will be no laughter,
only a black throat
digesting its tongue in silence.

Sometimes I think of sculptor's angels,
guardians of the fine lawns,
and how the wind
fights
to be free of the grass.

Turning the Corner for Home

Weathervanes stand like signposts
at the crossroads of the seasons.
Even here in the city
these past weeks
I've been able to divine in my bones
the least shift in the water table.
This humid August night when streetlamps smoke,
while everyone sleeps
I jog the streets alone.
The blue trees are heavy with dew,
and cicadas sing like the welts
a sandy-haired farm woman
once switched into my calves and thighs
for stealing from her orchard.
Even now as I give over each grain
of the body's worth
to the growing stain on my sweatshirt,
I somehow expect to find
those cool nectarines
awaiting my thirst after all these years,
shining on the draining board
in my dimly lit kitchen.

DRAWING A SEA-HORSE

You know better than I, Kristina,
When you say
The radiant spoonfuls
Of halved grapefruit we have for breakfast
Are pink topaz,
Or take up with such reverence
In the garden
A snail's shell
As if it were a miniature cupola.

For you the spider is a minstrel,
And a mantis
The devil's archbishop.
You keep in a brass box
A dead cricket
Like a fragment of a fallen star.

How easily a five-year-old grasps in the tines
Of a pine cone
The geometries of fire!

Tonight, as you stare into the fireplace,
Your crayon
Wandering over the white paper
Phosphorous,
And deliberate as a slug's trace
There emerges
A weary sea-horse,

Centurion of the cradled deep.

The Priest and the Toad

Where the toad lays its eggs like a living rosary,
They found them tangled in the hair
Of a child who drowned last week.
The priest hears the click of beads at Mass,
Memory flares in the curve of his nostril.
He sees tadpoles breathe like ecstatic notes,
A body burning in moonlit shallows.
Her touch would make the reeds shiver.
Of all children, this was the one he loved;
Now not even the bellying church organ
Could roll the stone from her grave.
Tonight, in blue clay where the worm
Works out a destiny of its own,
Her fresh plot exhales one toadstool.

ANGLER

Blue lettuce, tomato wedges,
Saltcellar, a cruet of salad oil.
He listens for her footfall
On the stairway,
The doorbell's lilt.
He sees the trout laid
On the draining board,
How the last ray of sun
Delights each scale.
Head, fins, and tail
Go to the knife.
The skillet cracks its fats.
The china's dealt,
Candles and phonograph
Set rippling.
He remembers a box
Of lures and tackle,
Hooks barbed like jewels.

REVEL

I remember my grandmother's wake,
The evening you slipped from her wizened
Finger a ruby brimming blood. I recall
The iced raisin-bread on the sideboard,
Mugs of black coffee cut with buckwheat
Honey and hot brandy, how I hoisted you
To the fiddle's cry and clarinet's bleating,
The arid bliss as I reeled in the warm
Flicker of your breathing. We had
No earthly desire to mend our sorrow,
And as your voice groped toward twilight
I took your lower lip between my teeth.
All night the creek by the cemetery
Braided and stitched—I imagined
Owls winking like lanterns in the woods.

A Blues Funeral Mood

There's a pall over the South
this September evening
thicker
than the blue haze of swank haunts in Memphis
where suddenly
the ribs are too greasy
and the beer flat
and loneliness
this two a.m. is like pawnshops boarded up
from Beale St.
to Bourbon
where the drummer like a charioteer
lets the reins go slack
over a team
of blooded saxophones
and shifting low
they carry us out over the wet cobbles
of the French Quarter
past nimbus-lit lampposts
and up two flights
to a room
where the lady with a Creole gaze
unfastens both teardrops
and places them
carefully on a varnished bureau
the clarinet cools down to a few
bleak embers
and the black widow embraces a moth
her scarlet lantern
faltering

WARM LATITUDES

I. Fayetteville, Memorial Day

Noon puts an icy glaze on wicker chairs
In the Ozarks; bees banded black and gold
Swarm the ruptured casks of watermelons.

At night rain pelts the fresh cadaver out
The reeking red clay-and-limestone of its plot.
Cataracts claw their way down from the heights.

When I take a back-alley home on foot,
I can hear antique fans beating the thick air,
Breathe deep the honeysuckle-rank odor

Of lovemaking. From second-story windows
Comes laughter, light, casual as a summer dress
And the muffled snigger of bed-springs . . .

II. The Crescent City, New Year's Eve

I remember a rain-slick night on Bourbon Street,
Bars drifting like luxury liners in the spillage
Of their colored lights. Breezes tinct with salt

From the Gulf swayed palms on the riverfront,
Rumpled the blue-and-white striped awning
Of Le Pavillon Hotel, where we stayed.

A Christmas fir stood in the lobby. We took
Dessert in our room, ruddy-skinned pears popped
With their own syrups. We left the window open

To new stars. I dreamed of a woman many floors
Below us, somehow radiant in her sorrow,
Wading the deep snows of the pianoforte.

James Bowie: Bexar, 1836

Into the chapel now withdrew the remnants
of the garrison. By most reports, Bowie himself
was sequestered in a side room, the baptistry.
            Lon Tinkle, *Thirteen Days to Glory*

From the shoals of Bowie's blear-eyed fever
Wade the Aldama chasseurs, pompoms nodding
Above black leather shakos like cattails
Along the Louisiana bayou. Stretched a fort-
Night on his cot in the tiny baptistry
Of the mission church, San Antonio
De Valero, burned out by aguardiente
And a slow siege of tuberculosis,
For him this is *la hora de la verdad.*
Except to pry loose for melting and molding
Into bullets the little leaden filigree
Ornaments from the window casings
Of the limestone Alamo chapel,
The big knife shackled to his fist by turn
On turn of a black-beaded rosary
Has thus far played no part in the battle.

Bowie's chest labors like a ribbed bellows,
And again coals shift and glow white-hot
In the forge of James Black, Arkansas cutler
And smith who battered from a fantail of sparks
The huge blade now rinsed with a bluish luster.
A guttering tallow-dip in the dying man's cell,
Its walls stuccoed white and trimmed with azure,
Pinions the shadow of his propped shoulders
Like wings of a bat. Leather-stropped or
Sweetened on soapstone, his craving to cut
And slake with the cool Damascus was native
To the welter of youth. It gave him a handle,
The ivory-hafted steel, a slick purchase

On a rival's whole basket of guts.
Stacks of poker chips burst over the green
Felt gaming tables of Natchez-on-the-Hill

As he squandered a paper fortune hard-wrung
From bog-trotting, cypress, sugar cane, and rum.
Wed to Veramendi's daughter, a beauty
Intricate as the floral scroll carved above
The arched portal of this crumbling edifice,
Bowie yoked to his star the vice-governor's
Palace. But nothing stays in the province
Of Coahuila-Texas. Land of scorpions,
Flint, and brick gouged out of yellow clay,
Each dwelling knows a subtle harmony
With earth, wind, and rain. Here *ancianos*
Weather the years like adobe, while cholera
Claims the young. Now Ursulita festers
In her shroud at Monclova and the groom
Listens to the brass notes of the "*Degüello*"
Buckle in the predawn air. Pageantry

Attends death, as well as life, in Bexar.
Consider the chapel's sculpted façade,
How the passionate torque of each column
Squeezes out a Corinthian capital, a stone
Acanthus withered by frost and shellfire.
Enter the sanctuary, the inner walls
Spattered and pocked, thick plaster rippling
With shot from the massed *escopetas:*
Trace the rich stains at every station
Of the cross. What harvest is forthcoming
As he watches from the delirium,
Hoping to lure into his gleaming arc
An officer whose epaulettes and frogging
Drip silver? Sabbath sun streaks the bayonets
And the brackish light begins to go.
Wind hushes in the cattails along the shore.

THE NATCHEZ SANDBAR FIGHT

Though he cannot know it at such an hour,
This is Major Norris Wright's time to atone,
The final daybreak to take in certain ravishments
Of the eye and delectations of the ear: the music
Of a porcelain basin poured to the brim, a mauve-handled
Straight razor and frothing mug of mint-scented
Lather laid out for his morning's ritual laving
And whisking away of a night's crisp stubble.
He squires himself into silken white sleeves,
Securing each mother-of-pearl button
With the deftness of one who's master
Of the pasteboards, prestidigitator
Fanning a pat hand, spades and hearts,
A peacock beneath chandeliers spilling crystal
And nickel. Before quitting his chambers, he lifts
From a box two snub-nosed pistols slumbering in velvet,
Then reaches for his ivory-knobbed sword cane:
Jim Bowie would later gasp on the Natchez sandbar,
Sped through the lung with its slender yard
Of watery steel. But a terrible grip would close
On Wright's subtle wrist, his shoulder's bone-
Lappings keening as he strove to pull away. The
Interval was Bowie's. His whetted Damascus
Cut the major free of both liver and lights
There in the sun-stunned blaze of a Delta noon,
The hour of no shadow when the wounded
And dead seem borne aloft on the gnat-swarming air,
And flocking sparrows grit up, filling their crops
With sweet sticky gobbets of warm sand.

BONHAM ON THE NIGHT PRAIRIE

Deep gashes of vermilion and gold welter
Along the horizon; in the full onslaught
Of evening, James Butler Bonham
Drops a feral hog with one shoulder-shot
From his father's fifty-caliber Hawken—
Lacking time to unseam and field dress
The matted tusker, he carves out a haunch
With his Green River butcher knife,
And soon a cudgel of pork thigh
Crackles and spits as the fat runs
Over a fire of dry mesquite, bedded
Embers pulsing like stars in the night heavens.
What auspicious signs here converge,
As the weary Alamo courier stares
Into a veritable abyss of living coals,
Mindful of urgent missives that line
His deerskin saddlebags, appeals for aid
To Gonzales, Goliad, and San Felipe?
Thirty miles from San Antonio de Bexar,
He rode out when Mexican howitzers
Unlimbered and lobbed the first shells
Into the compound of sun-cured mud
And quarried limestone. Now utter silence
As lightning, viper-tongued, licks around,
A storm or some other perilous
Circumstance amaking to the west,
Although the east is sprent with stars
And hope yet abides in its tiny settlements.
Bonham closes his eyes, once, twice—
Listens to his hobbled Appaloosa nicker
Only a few yards away, fang-bared wolves
Snarling in the distance over the boar's
Scattered entrails. Tomorrow he will clop
Into the dusty streets of Gonzales, but for now
He gazes deep within, seeking always

A portent, any nebulous glimmer
Still suspended in delicate equipoise
Amid the dark's listing firmament.
A meteor goes rifling down the void.

TRAVIS

I. The Hewn Log House: Claiborne, Alabama

Hefting the shrewd-edged broadax for hours
Until a felled poplar was a beam hewn
Flush and smooth on four sides, a youth's
Torso slowly hardened into paneled oak.
The hollow gourd went to the barrel and back,
As Buck took his turn at a crosscut saw.
To avoid curling, cedar shakes were split
While the moon was on the wax, and peat moss
Culled for chinking drank many times
Its weight in moisture. Dovetail notches
Linked the logs at each corner. Creek stones
Bedded in lime mortar formed a chimney.
William Barret Travis lay by the fireplace,
Hearing salvos of bullfrogs and gators
Diminish along the starlit backwaters
Of Mobile. White-bellied mosquitos
Imbibed from his veins the sticky humors
As he dreamed a future written in blood.

II. Rough Justice

His clan traversed the wagon-rutted road
From Edgefield County, a South Carolina
Tract dubbed Pandemonium or Abode
Of the Devils. By candlelight he got
A smattering of Latin and Greek,
Spilling more tallow in the loft by day
With Rosanna Cato. Married at nineteen,
Already he sat his black Spanish mare
Like a Cossack. Firing a sawed-off
Shotgun slung over his pommel kicked
The idle heart back to life: he loved the jolt
Of Anabaptist thunder, the sulfurous

Prickle that belled both nostrils. Spellbinder
And rhetorician, preferring the law
To the pulpit, one night he recast
Its letter in the shape of a spent ball.
He cited Rosanna's trifling, his skill
With a pistol, as reasons for a stranger's fall.

III. Command of the Alamo: February 24, 1836

His pen nib like a falcon's beak, horn-sheathed
And honed slick, seeking always to tap
The heart of the unborn republic, he scrawled
Bombast for an age of Byron and Scott
While the Mexican howitzers lobbed
Grenades into the compound: "To the People
Of Texas and all Americans in the World—."
So much for the quill-tip trimmed and slit,
The alchemy of words scripted in severe
Loops and swirls. He saw dragoons in brass
And steel glitter along the Alazan Heights,
Heard sappers' spades tongue gritty earth
As entrenchments nudged closer. A keepsake
For the dispossessed, his cat's-eye ring
Of beaten gold he threaded and dangled
About Angelina Dickinson's neck. Specters
Loomed in the tabernacle of his skull,
A votive nub winked in the chapel all night.

IV. The Final Assault: Five A.M., March 6, 1836

From the north battery, his cannon's spout
Spewed bits of chain and chopped horseshoes
Wailing down rank on rank of the Toluca
Battalion. The cry of advancing columns
Shattered the empyrean, and he stood
Silhouetted one moment above the ramparts
Hearing the syllables of his name leap

As he unsheathed the sabre at his side.
A blind volley broke the cluster of veins
At his temple, and he plummeted,
Brain-struck archangel, from the walls
Into grace: "*No rendirse, muchachos!*"
He called to men in Seguin's detachment
As the dull missile met his forehead,
Unsettling continents of bone. Where the hot
Lead cooled the blood congealed like wax.
His fate sealed, Travis saw the planet tilt,
Slow smoke unroll from the mission's rubble.

Alamo Pyre: March 6, 1836

Soldiers layered the pyres with wood and kindling,
then bodies, then more wood, kindling, then bodies.
Jeffery Long, *Duel of Eagles*

Like brightly plumed fighting cocks in a pit,
The first flames to crest the pyre buffet and flap,
Fall back. Stacked northeast of La Villita,
Scrub oak and mesquite in layers, then
A row of corpses, a few bled so white
Their bones shine like ivory tapers lit
Beneath the vaulted dome of San Fernando.
No incantation here, no Pentecostal blaze,
Not even the *rogus* of ancient Rome:
This is the heretic's fire steepled, forking
Here and there among the branches
Of hacked and splintered chaparral. Crockett's
Buckskin fringe sizzles, then twines blue smoke
Like a cache of duds. Heat begins to raze
The lightly downed cheek of Carlos Espalier:
Protégé to Bowie, on feast days he rode
Down Calle Durango like an emperor
Bestowing on all the imperial nod.
After the battle, the Vera Cruz fusiliers
Sheared from his leggings the silver buttons,
Stripped his leather boots of the gringo spurs.
Before daybreak they had riddled out
His life's mystery at bayonet point;
Now the fire sputters and pops, feeding
His resinous heart. The sticky sap
Seethes in his loins; tendons and cartilage
Whine as the bones pull apart. Santa Anna
Paces in a striped marquee, waiting to crush
Beneath his heel the last filibuster spark.

CROCKETT

The Colonel had found an old fiddle somewhere, and he
would challenge McGregor to get out his bagpipes to see
who could make the most noise.
Walter Lord, *A Time to Stand*

The coonskin cap some purists vow he never wore,
Bristles in firelight as he carves out
On his fiddle a Celtic air, and the little
Ring-tailed scrapper gone blind with the rage
Of gazing inward emblazons the span
Above his brow. In the shadow of the slab-
Sided chapel, a spitted ox bastes and seethes,
Cornbread crackles in an iron skillet. Crockett
Surrendered, they now say, and Santa Anna's
Gleaming entourage cut him down as tailors
Would a legend grown too large. The steel
Was still smoking when they resheathed
The swords with basket-hilts of inlaid silver.
Mrs. Dickinson would later remember
His corpse amid the other carnage
In the courtyard, how the "peculiar cap"
Lay by Crockett's side. Whether or not
Its glossy nap yet stirred with the deathless
Saga of the Canebrake Congressman is unknown—
But conjure him once, his face stained
With the low-banked fires of the Alamo Plaza,
The fiddle braced under his chin, the slender
Arm dancing out and in, while McGregor's pipes
Bleat like newborn kids on a swollen udder.

CROCKETT BY FIRELIGHT

To thwart the evening chill, John Crockett
Would draw a deep tankard of his own stock
From an oak-staved cask. A leather-aproned
Tavern host grown stout with memory
Of wielding the flintlock pegged above the bar
At the battle of King's Mountain, he often
Took the measure of his stripling son
With a birch rod. Young David never chafed

At splitting fence rails with maul and wedge,
But when his father sent him to scratch
A slate at the age of twelve, he bolted.
Now he hunkers by firelight in the chalk-white
Glow of the limestone chapel, his name
A legend in columns back East. An iron horse
Hitched to a congregation of vapors,
The *Davy Crockett* beats its way

From Saratoga to Schenectady
Belching a cloud of sparks. Crockett closes
His eyes a moment, rides the cool
Slipstream of twenty-five miles an hour
Beneath the stars of the old republic.
Yet he prefers the tall chestnut mare
With the blaze on her forehead. She bore
His raw-boned bulk from Gibson County

To San Antonio, helped him escape
The industrial reek of the seaboard states,
Whig intrigue, the glib political
Machine of Jackson's Kitchen Cabinet,
Inexorable gears that notch and wheel,
Grinding the common man to bonemeal.
Stump oratory came easy at first,
Each ballot like a glimmering perch

Snatched from a millrace with the hook
Of native wit. But Crockett's constituency
Went straight to hell at the August polls.
Before the ripe persimmons fumed
In a killing frost and the black bear gorged,
He struck out for Texas, the bluestem prairies
Rolling away under the hooves of buffalo.
He forsook "Pretty Betsey," the engraved

Pennsylvania rifle inlaid with gold
And German silver, a weapon shaped
By the gods of covetousness. He chose
Instead his percussion muzzle-loader,
Its copper nipple, and the smoke-smudged
Sights that gleam no warning. Tonight
He fed his fire in the Alamo courtyard
A shoot of resinous cedar; an ember popped,

Leapt the flames, and lit like a flea on the toe
Of his boot: "Lice and such varmints as these
Always quit a dying man," he observed,
"I'm good for a few years yet." Others roared,
But he swallowed like it was hard medicine.
A seraphic ghoul resplendent in frock coat
And bullion tassels, Santa Anna offered
A battalion of *fusileros* for slaughter

Nine days ago. How many yeoman-crowned
Bullhide shakos did Crockett topple
Between the mud-chinked *jacales* south
Of the mission outworks? Before the sun
Turns the evening mist to blood-red dawn
He foresees a full-scale assault. A torch
Spindles and wisps near the low barracks wall.
Women and children dream on burnished straw.

GREGORIO ESPARZA

Although a member of Seguin's company, Esparza helped
man a cannon in the Alamo chapel where his wife and
children were sheltered.

William Groneman, *Alamo Defenders*

At the cusp of summer, amid mayflies,
Herons patrol the reedy, milk-jade shallows
Of the San Antonio, their necks recurved
Bows darting at minnows. Tomatoes,
Squash, onions, figs, wild mustang grapevines
Thrive in Gregorio Esparza's garden.
On the acequia's east bank, his two-room
Adobe breathes with the earth, its cool,
Dry interior hung with strings of red
And yellow peppers: "Of food, we had
Not overmuch—beans and chili, chili
And beans . . . but there was time to work and rest
And look at growing plants." Winter grips
Bexar, effacing the arid landscape,
And the hairy hand of a tarantula
Fiddles at the latch. Dolorous hooves
Toll along the stony Camino Real,
As Santa Anna's mounted vanguard
Enters the barren northern provinces
Like a cold wind from Ecclesiastes.

In February, the Centralist eagles
Cross the Medina: Esparza casts his lot
With the insurgents in the old mission,
Hoisting by rope and pulley onto a scaffold
In the apse of the church a terrible
Deus ex machina, the iron tube
A Spanish twelve-pounder adorned
With twin dolphins. Thirteen days he abides

Aloft this makeshift ramp. His *niño* Enrique
Shrinks from flames, the crumping roar
Of the three-piece battery. Like Dickinson,
He keeps wife and children close,
Fingering his beads on the rainy evening
When Juan Seguin lays his scourge
Against the racing flanks of Bowie's sorrel,
And vanishes down the Gonzales Road.
The big knife-fighter, Don Santiago,
Tosses on a cot in the low barracks:
Leeches batten on the fever in his blood.
Doc Pollard drags hard, sears them off

With the smoldering ash of a cigar.
Esparza's cannon broaches the night air,
And as sparks shower the platform,
He knows how futile his attempt
To break the generalissimo's hold.
The siege tightens: a mineral sweat
Lurks in the limestone walls by day,
Making the chapel dank as a sepulchre.
Catcalls drift across the river each twilight,
Words so serenely murderous they
Raise the hackles at Gregorio's nape.
He sees men crouch around watchfires
In the Alamo compound, silence
And shadow the only realities
During a lull. One Anglo knocks lead
From a pincer mold, another whets
An Arkansas toothpick on the sole
Of his boot. Like a peasant girl
From her rebozo, the moon peers down.
The assault columns edge into place.

KENTUCKY LONG RIFLES

In the buttstock of polished maple,
A hinged cavity hid the greasy, square-cut
Linen patches that wrapped each leaden ball,
Easing it along spiral grooves engraved
The barrel's length. Tamped home against
A sixty-grain charge, the snug fit between slug
And rifling formed a gas seal, boosting
Pressure and velocity. From dun walls
On the sunrise side of the river, a poised
Sniper could spill the eye of a gold-braided
Zapadore at two hundred paces. Saxon
Gutturals lit the powder train when flint
Kissed steel, and many a rebel lived
An eternity in the abrupt snarl
And flare of the hangfire. His jaw
Swollen with a quid of tobacco,
Admiring the clean-run, equestrian
Grace of Sesma's dragoons, Crockett
Sighted along the earth-rammed palisade
Between the chapel and low barracks,
Squeezing off round after round. Twelve days
The Army of Operations kept a distance
From the Alamo's crumbling redoubts.
Silver cartwheels rang every night
In the *pulquerías* and brothels,
Candles spent like profligates in reed-
Thatched *jacales* east of town. Violin,
Guitar, and cornet: eleven evenings
Of revelry, though Kentucky long rifles
Showed His Excellency each morning
How Texas cut the pigeon's wing.

KENTUCKY GUNSMITH: LONG RIFLE, 1833

Blacksmith, mechanic, wood-sculptor, jeweler:
He begins in the forge, wrapping a pressed bar
Of wrought iron braced on a swage block
With ringing triple skelps of his hammer
Around a mandril rod. He sinks the lap-welded
Barrel in a ticking bed of gold and blue
Bituminous embers, letting it cool
And set before he wrests the metal free
With tongs and bears it smoking like hoarfrost
To the anvil, where he batters out the flats,
Eight sides, up and down its length.
He bores smooth the octagonal tube, then rifles it—
Hickory shims set behind steel cutting teeth
Deepen the grooves with each successive pass.

He fashions lock and plate piece by piece.
Consigning frizzen, fly, tumbler, and springs
To the crucible, he threads the breech plug
And draws the glowing tang sharp as a prong:
A forked vein pulses in his temple,
His eyes glaze and crack with blood.
Before sand-casting both muzzle-cap
And butt plate in brass, he retrieves
And quenches the parts of tempered steel.
The heat-refracted shed recedes
Like a mirage, as he walks the sixteen furlongs
To the Morgan Whitehackle Inn.
The tavern host slides a tall schooner
Of amber-lit ale across the polished board.

Thoughts steeped in seasoned grains, he savors
The barley-bree, mulling texture and hue,
Chopped heartwood of curly maple

Planed smooth with a drawknife. He returns
To the shop, traces on a cured slab the rude
Template of his stock. His gouge and drill-bit
Drop ringlets and curls. He cuts the lugs,
Seats the barrel, tests the ramrod groove.
Rasp and file embalm the air, as he raises
Cheekpiece and comb on the buttstock.
He endows the wrist with a slender turn,
Chisels a rib to secure lock, cock, frizzen,
And ignition pan. He blocks out a cavity
For the springworks, assembles the hardware,

And next a pillar of blazing sawdust motes
He starts to carve in earnest. Virtuosity
In the pursuit of form lies in slickest
Evasion. Everything flows, sinuous
Lines holding plane and mass forever
In the present tense. The stock tapers
And flares all the barrel's length. He raises
In low relief a baroque C-scroll behind
The cheekpiece. Above the vent-pick eyelets
He incises a garfish and taps the glyph
Full of relic silver. He chases
Rime-encrusted florals, stars, and sickle moons
Along the tang and breech. He files
Diamond facets into the ramrod thimbles

And redeems in linseed oil the sculpture's
Tiger-striped grain. Spurning always
The nacreous tints of fresh-water pearl,
For inlay he chooses ivory worried
From the jawbone of Pleistocene cave bear,
Ferocious canines arcing slow meteors
Either side of the forestock. Thirty months
The sun fails beautifully on beaten sheet brass,
The hinged patch box cunningly embellished

As a gilt frame in a New Orleans parlor—
Until Daniel William Cloud, 24 years old,
Bound for rebellion in the Texas province,
Puts down ten Coronet gold eagles, swings up
By the left stirrup, and boots his horse toward Bexar.

BERSERKER

Acrid fumes of charred brimstone
Assail the thronging San Luis *cazadores*
As they clamber up timbers bracing
The Alamo's shell-eroded north wall.

Colonel Amat's sappers attack with pick
And crowbar the lime-washed adobe bricks
That now seal the west-facing window
Of the Treviño house. Exhorting others

To follow, a young officer, his tunic front
Scintillant as a glockenspiel, vaults
The sepia-toned rubble. It proves
Daunting to fall back, to seat with sweat-

Crawling palms a lead ball in a muzzle-loader.
Northcross unbuckles his shotgun belt,
Strips the packed leather tube from his back—
Plugging in turn each barrel with a brass spout

He wrings the pellets home like a butcher
Pouring gravel from a goose's crop.
Cocking and leveling, he blasts a fusilier
Heaving a gleaming short sword

From under his shako's yellow raquettes
And cording. Sternum shattered and ribcage
Sprung, the luckless *soldado* never hears
The sleeting double thump. He closes his eyes

On candescent barrels roiling like blowflies.
Someone bellows in a dark corner
Of the mission's long barracks, a man
Who has earned the bear-shirt, the berserker's

Keening blood-wail; he flails enrapt
The burst crown of his empty powder horn,
Smashing jaws hard-set and crammed with molars,
Rupturing the frail sutures of every skull.

SANTA ANNA'S SPURS

for George Core

I. Mexico City: The Street of the Artisans, 1834

Not the hammer with its deft sure stroke,
But the anvil, blue-black as a meteorite,
Rings home the shaping of steel. The smith, by dint
Of sheer will, forges from hoar-white metal
Heel, shank, and rowel, the spur perfect
For quickening the glossy flanks of any stallion,
Putting the proudest horseflesh on its mettle.
This is the Calle Plateros, Mexico City,
Circa 1834. *El Presidente* seeks out
An artisan of yet finer touch, desiring
For the heel a gold-inlaid band exquisitely
Engraved with trailing vines. Next, he locates
A man that knows the raw whiff and burn
Of everyday toil, a craftsman who works
In hand-tooled leather; Santa Anna wants
Straps he can wear buckled on the inside
To show off conchos of purest silver.

II. San Antonio de Bexar: March 5-6, 1836

Against the backdrop of a westering sun
Almost lost behind the Alazan Heights,
Each radiant of the generalissimo's rowel
Suddenly flares as the man himself is cast
Into silhouette; the drawn moderation
Of his lean profile belies the caprice
That will crush beneath his boot heel,
Like a dirt-clod, the adobe battlements
Of the Alamo before dawn.
                                    In darkness,

Around watchfires, rebels of determined mien
Run balls and cut patches for long rifles—
They grease little swatches of cloth
In fat fleeced from slaughtered steers,
Cross-notch each leaden orb so it shatters
Human bone on impact. Soon come
The fiery strains of the *"Degüello,"*
The flames' liquefaction and crackling
Among thatched hovels along the west wall.
Rank on rank, fusils level and ignite,
Spouting sulfurous jets, as Mexican battalions
Carry the compound with shot and bayonet.

First light hardens to translucent horn
In the silent chancel of the roofless church.
Maimed *soldados* lie in field hospitals
Calling out for *Maria, Madre de Dios;*
Captain Juan Sanchez Navarro declares,
"Another such victory will ruin us."

III. Mexico City: September, 1847

Big roweled spurs: the mark of the *caballero.*
Santa Anna cannot do other than hearken
To the tingle and whir of his booted striding
Down corridors of state. This morning,
He must surrender to General Winfield Scott,
Who returns his sword worth seven thousand pesos.
Not to be outdone, gesture for gesture,
The *caudillo* unbuckles and bestows
His gold-mounted spurs on the grizzled *norte.*
Pride in his estate called Manga de Clavo—
Spike of the Clove at red-tiled Jalapa—
And his fighting cocks of burnished feather,
Clings like a burr for years to come.

IV. Mexico City, 1847-Appomatox, 1865

Scott broods on the spurs' gilt pattern,
Imagining a dew-soaked vineyard fanning out
Like the first rays of sun. He remembers
Mexico City's great cathedral, its
Soaring vaults and silver altar rails,
The carved *santos*, their painted robes
Set with rubies, sapphires, and topaz—
Beneath loose wooden floorboards lay
Old corruption and dead men's bones,
The mingling of magnificence and squalor
To Scott's Protestant reckoning a legacy
Of priest-vested despots down the ages.

The general sits at his portable escritoire,
An alabaster lamp laps oil. Caring little
For the spoils of war, he will award the spurs
To Benjamin Huger, his youthful captain
Of ordnance and artillery, citing valor
At Vera Cruz, Chapultepec, Molino del Rey.
The spurs become heirlooms when Huger
Presents them to his son on graduation
From West Point. Officer in the Norfolk
Light Artillery, Frank Huger stands by his brass
Smoothbore Napoleons at Fredericksburg,
Reaping the advancing Federal lines
With grapeshot and canister. Captured
Near Appomattox, he lends the spurs
To his old classmate, George Armstrong Custer—
Thus, they fall into the hands of another cavalier.

V. The Little Bighorn: June 25, 1876

Custer delights in each chinking heel-strike,
Deems the spurs fit plunder for a brigadier,
And forgets the staid gunner with whom
He shared a sterling hip flask at the Point.

Like Santa Anna, he owns the habit
Of contempt, mistaken for flamboyance
By those who admire his navy-blue tunic
And flowing red cravat, the buckskin jacket

Worn despite the swelter and haze, his brow
Popped with sweat beneath a Montana sun.
Rolling drums and skirling fifes brazen out
"Garry Owen," making his scalp go taut

And prickle as he goads his sorrel forward—
The swallow-tailed guidons of the Seventh
Flutter and snap. The regimental band stays
At Powder River depot; all sabres have been

Crated up and the pine lids nailed shut.
No martial airs or clanking steel must alert
The Sioux and Northern Cheyenne. Crow scouts
Spy a vast herd of grazing ponies and warn

The Son of the Morning Star—how he relishes
The epithet—to look for "worms in the grass."
He plunges down Medicine Tail Coulee,
And strikes the middle of a sprawling camp

Two miles long, his last message a scrawl:
"Benteen. Big village. Be quick. Bring packs."
Five companies perish among the hills
And gullies, Custer's ivory-handled

English Webley bulldogs banging off
Cylinder after cylinder before he falls,
A rifle ball lodged under his ribcage.
He lies back, amazed by a painted arrow's

Slow arc, the ecstatic hover and plummet
To earth, like a hawk stooping on its prey.
As his grey eyes film and his gaze dries,
He has no thought for the Alamo garrison

Burned to glory on mass pyres forty years ago,
Or the *caudillo*, dead just three weeks past,
Returned from exile to Mexico, his last days
Lived out, serene, in solitude and poverty.

THE FRUITS OF VICTORY

Halley's comet: the year of the broom-star.
Santa Anna swept the northern provinces
Clear of homesteaders within twelve months.
Saddle-notched dogtrot cabins, hewn heartwood
Blazed in Gonzales till the least ember
Hissed to a standstill amid charred wreckage.

Nearer the Sabine, barns bulged with cotton
Ginned and carded; bludgeons of pork thigh
Swung from smokehouse rafters, bacon slabs
Carved thick as psalters cured in a cryptic blue.
Plunder was abundant: beeswax, white sugar,
Bitter chocolate, mirrors, clocks, whiskey.

One-fourth of the Toluca Battalion
Leavened the sunbaked graves at Bexar.
That frozen, cirrus-misted night in March
They had perished by the squad as Travis's
Cannon bucked, hurling shrapnel from the north-
West wall. The Campo Santo could not hold

Their sum. Corpses drifted in the suck
And sway as the purling San Antonio made
Crisp gashes breathe like gills. Santa Anna
Pondered stippled trout, the hummingbirds
Of the South. From the lava-rich tropics
To the high chaparral, he embodied it all.

Green rind, white quick, red core—like a silken
Tricolor—watermelon would split open
At one swift stroke of the *caudillo's* sword.
He dreamed of his estates at Jalapa,
El Presidente, dozing in his pavilion
While the columns groped toward San Jacinto.

Degüello

Islamic Moors first sounded the "cut-throat" song
In Spain, its fiery strains recasting each bugle
In tones of molten brass. It summoned death
And decay, the mephitic vapors of a wound
Left untended for days. When Santa Anna's
Regimental bands swelled the Mexican advance,
The Texas hardpan quaked like an Arab drum,
The Alamo fell to the glint of fixed bayonets.
Scored notes: grenadiers marching *en punto*.
Dawn trumpet bleeding down the gauze-streaked sky.

ERIC VON SCHMIDT: BEYOND CANVAS

In Von Schmidt's *The Storming of the Alamo*,
It's a half-hour since the trumpets brayed
Columns of *soldados*, crouched in a dark field
Of trampled maize, to their feet and forward
To the north wall of glazed, shell-pocked adobe
Braced by packed earth and rough-shorn timbers.
Pumped into a sky still popped with stars,
Flares illuminate the plaza as William Carey
Gouges with the vent-pick on his thumb
The powder bag rammed fast to the breech
Of his cannon, and drives a priming tube
Into the charge. Coiled with a slow fuse,
No doubt his twinkling linstock trembles
Grafting fire to black grain. The big gun rolls,
Disgorging into the Aldama Battalion twelve pounds
Of searing iron links. Caught in a flank maneuver,
The field manual's smart right oblique,
Did *los jovenes* remember the camp gypsy,
The gut-thumping membrane, the quick sizzle
Of her tambourine, as the shrapnel
Cut a swath through their serried ranks?
But the elite *Zapadores* climb up
The patched redoubt, its chinks and uneven
Beam ends, spilling over onto the parapet.
Carey pauses to crush with a handspike
The temporal bone beneath a dragoon's
Helmeted brow. The acrid snap and tongued flame
Of a smoothbore ignite his woolen jacket—
Like knives at a spit, the bayonets probe.

THE MILITIA SHIRT

Even as the Gonzales Ranging Company
Set out for the Alamo on the afternoon
Of February 27, 1836, fifteen-year-old
William Phillip King caught the reins
Of Captain Kimball's nutmeg roan
And begged leave to go in his father's stead.
He had nine younger siblings. Let someone
Sturdier follow the double yoke of oxen
Pulling the long furrow toward sundown.
Kimball shrugged; his rump firmly settled
In the hull of a new Ringgold saddle,
He nodded reluctant assent, his long rifle's
Feather-grained cherrywood riding
Easy in the crook of his arm. King's mother
Had nightmares all the coming week:
The old mission chapel's ornate façade
Obscured in the particle haze and sulfurous
Reek of powder smoke, her firstborn
Fighting for his life with a Green River
Butcher knife rehafted in elkhorn. Every day
Her spinning wheel ran with the sun,
And each night she sat at her loom
Weaving threads into whole fabric.
She had cut and sewn the chamber-dyed
Militia shirt, biting back loose strands
Like cries of grief. Now she saw a *cazadore's*
Double-edged sword bayonet burst
The fascia of William's abdomen,
Glutinous red drink the rough butternut
Cloth of linen warp and woolen weft.

AFTERMATH: DUSK AT THE ALAMO

John Purdy Reynolds sprawls before the chapel's
Blood-spattered façade, its earth tones
Of burnt umber and raw sienna no longer
Beguiling his every glance. Indeed, the town
Of San Antonio, the white-washed adobes
And dwellings of hewn limestone, conjured
For many a footloose garrison bravo
A New World Judea. A little beyond the river,
Sun-spangled at the gravel-barred ford,
Stood the shantytown of La Villita with its onyx-
Eyed *señoritas*; here the fare was often plain—
Tamales wrapped in corn shucks, pulque
Sipped from jars of unfired clay—but each night
Reynolds lay in one girl's casual embrace,
Moonlight seeping through the chinked *jacale*,
A cricket in the thatch like a bell of black tin.
Now an ashen haze has settled over the mission
This chill sabbath, and his Kentucky-wrought
Smoke pole no longer shoots for gold braid.
In the lapel of his blue swallow-tailed coat
Hot lead spun off the lands and grooves
Of a Baker rifle fired from the west wall
Left a boutonnière of caked blood
Where the fatal round plunked home.
Straight as a bride a solitary figure moves
Among the rebels in the hour before twilight,
Seeking out one soul of all the dead:
From a countenance curiously serene
She wipes thick battle-grime and flecked gore,
Placing the soaked kerchief between her breasts.
Tumbrils groan, rolling corpses to bonfires.

SAN ANTONIO DE VALERO

I. The Mission Period: Antonio de Tello

In the Year of Our Lord, seventeen hundred
And fifty-six, master artisan
Antonio de Tello, having served
A full apprenticeship peeling limestone
With mallet and chisel, carving rosettes,
Grape clusters, acres of gothic fretwork,
Having observed the heresies of the Moorish
Influence right down to a snail's tiny mosque,
Gathers his well-honed tools and sets off
For the province of *Tejas,* there to transpose
The façade of the mission chapel
Near the reed-choked banks of the San Antonio
From a frowning mass to a marvel
Of Tuscan form. Yet the good friars

Care less for high artifice than the souls
Of *los Yndios Reducidos.* The curate
Locks pubescent converts, male and female,
Into separate cells every night
With eagle-headed keys of cold iron.
Several millennia before sparks leapt
As rapacious Apaches chipped free
A new ballistics slumbering in the core
Of igneous rock; now the adobe walls
And rough-hewn pueblo of the compound
Thwart the heathen's obsidian-tipped arrows.
Antonio waits two years for the ornate
Keystone to be set and blessed. After all,
Sculpture is an art of subtraction: better add

Stripe upon stripe to the backs of neophytes
Than cut twisted columns from the west
Face of the brooding Alamo. His St. Clare

Betrays in each contour the nubile grace
Of an onyx-eyed girl who grinds maize
In the kitchens. The scallop-shaped
Niche remains empty, and the cherished
Commission is revoked. Soon children dub
Antonio *El Borrachón* as he reels
About Bexar in the fumes of popskull
Caribbean rum. The padres bury him
In the earthen floor of the nave, just beyond
The sacristy's groined vault. Already
Groundwater is rising through porous stone.

II. Gone to Texas: Micajah Autry

Booking passage on the steamboat *Pacific*
One evening in early December 1835,
Micajah Autry scarcely envisions
His death before the blood-spackled façade
Of Antonio's deft conceiving, how he
And a beleaguered few would rally
In the shadow of that ruined proscenium
With no thought for the plaudits of the many,
The vast afflatus of the *Telegraph and
Texas Register*: "Spirits of the mighty,
Though fallen! Honors and rest are with ye."
Smoke batting its tall stacks, the stern-wheeler
Churns the Mississippi midchannel,
The moon shattered gypsum in its wake.

III. The 1836 Siege: Micajah Autry

Micajah owns a rich tenor voice, a sheaf
Of unpublished verse. He joins Crockett
On the long trek to Bexar, where the garrison
Scorns drill, holds formations in the cantina—
Almeron Dickinson, a blacksmith from Tennessee,
Forges horseshoes on a twin-pronged anvil.

Micajah savors the hammer's rhythmic pitch,
The prolonged hiss as incandescent iron
Cools out of its element to a new hardness:
Were words ever so malleable, so concise?
But winter settles in, cold and drizzling,
No time for poetry. At forty-two,
His thighbone grips his knee like fire tongs.
The weather eases up within a week.

Micajah shuns fandangos, and quarters
In the Alamo. Each night he guards
The horses cut out to graze on dry mesquite.
Three days before Santa Anna's arrival,
A ripple runs through the *caballada*,
The eyes of mustangs opalescent fire
Beneath the Comanche moon. Such portents
Go unheeded, till Bonham spurs in
From La Bahía, his Appaloosa
Blown and lathered, slick with yeasty silver.
Travis replies to the demand for surrender
With a cannon shot; the eighteen-pounder's
Bull-throated roar breaks and rolls like thunder—
Even at Washington-on-the-Brazos.

Politicians bickering in conclave
Pause to listen. But you knew, Micajah,
Didn't you, in the pith and marrow
Of your bones, that no relief column
Would move toward Bexar? On March first,
When thirty men slip the icy fetters
Of Cibolo Creek and follow the starlit
Acequia to the south gate, Travis
Slits an ox's throat to honor the town
Of Gonzales, searing the chine and joints
Over flame-gutted sticks of poplar.
That night Micajah partakes of eternity
As he crouches in a weathered portico
On the plaza. Ramon Caro, official

Secretary to His Supreme Excellency,
Would later call the Alamo "a mere
Corral, and nothing more." In the predawn
Haze and powder smoke of the final battle
Micajah falls back on the chapel,
His shotgun charged with blue whistlers
That cut a young *soldado's* plain coatee
To gaudy regimentals. The poet's breath
Catches in his beard, his right lung crumpled
By a musket ball: a bayonet gleans
The remnant, a twitch like phantom
Nerves in a severed limb. All afternoon
The Jimenez *cazadores* trundle
Cartloads of rebel corpses to pyres

Heaped on the Alameda. At last
The sun relents, melting down the brass
Shield insignia of bullrush-tufted shakos.
Parched and weary *soldados* loosen
And slough their glittering chin scales.
One by one, with a blazing pitch pine knot
The bonfires are lit, the wind springs up . . .

Columns of smoke and heat-flaked bone stand in heaven.

EXPIATION

for Teresa Shuler

Still in our teens we walked the back paths
Of Overton Park, looking for a place,
The cider-tart odor of crab apples
Underfoot in the time of falling leaves.
I am haunted a half-century later by the lovely
Apparition of her face, the numinous
Ever-recurring almost nightly visitation
That frequents my troubled sleep, defying
All wakeful attempts to exorcise the memories
Of what receded so long ago. It remains,
That brief season that transpired in another age,
And years pass, deepening with time the fallen
Leaves of red and gold along lost ways that yet beguile.

Farewell

She died in the days before the autumn equinox,
Twenty-five years after our short liaison
Of adolescent bravura and stealth played out
Along wooded trails. Caught up in the masque
And pageant of the turning season, cool mornings
We uttered endearments a bit too clipped
For the particle vapor that issued from our lungs,
Frost dispersing above the tree line pyrotechnic
With color. Now she lies beneath the cold sod
Of Murray, Kentucky, in a coffin once shining
And upholstered like a new roadster. Pallbearers
Filed past the casket at graveside, each placing
On its lid a boutonnière blue as a robin's egg.
Oblivious to that untimely aneurysm, the ripe berry
Of blood that burst in her brain, I slumbered as the stars
Of the Milky Way wandered the disheveled clouds.
Too many years since our parting had intervened;
Another man's ring encircles her desiccated finger,
And she, too, sleeps on a little past the dream.

THE VISITATION

The night she died without my knowledge
Was a cool evening in mid-September;
Frost had not yet turned the cricket's heart
To silver. But what vexed sleep was the owl,
The grey-tufted harbinger who refused
To shuffle its feathers once and slumber
The whole night through upon its perch
In the black oak beyond the creek. When
I was finally able to pillow my head
In oblivion, she stood before me
As in life: her short gypsy shag
Yellow as a hayrick, the jade ring
I once gave her now worn like a trinket
About her neck. Her silence was eloquent
As any speech: it spoke of bitter loss,
And an infinite yearning for peace at our touch.

Sleeping Over on Highway 78

for Richard Wooten

Thirty miles to the small town of Red Banks,
The phosphor-lit dial of your Opel Kadett's
Dashboard clock ticking out ten after ten,
A light rain intermittently stippling
The windshield with petti-tricolor drops
Smudged the next instant by the wipers'
Metronomic sway and rock,
Our antenna homing on Brenton Wood's
"Gimme Little Sign"; stars wandering
In a cirrus mist, we listen for the cricket
Scrabble in live bait shops, gold neon Jax
Blinking in the windows of darkened roadhouses
All along kudzu-hung Old Highway 78.

You brake hard, Rick, on the slow grade below
The trailer of red corrugated tin, the little
Dome light tricks on when both doors
Swing wide, and we can hear the chert
Cracking under our boot-heels striding up
The wet gravel drive. Your mother, already
In her housecoat, rises from a wicker-backed
Kitchen chair, fetching out of the Frigidaire
Frosted glass goblets brimming apple cider.
Before heading for the paneled bedroom
We spin a Jr. Walker side, then turn in,
Each dreaming about her blue eyes,
Autumn rain pelting us to who-knows-where.

THE YEARS BETWEEN

I watch the watery pitch of a black vinyl
33 rpm graduate in ripples from the center
Like an oak's heartwood, diamond tip
Needle threading the eddying current where

The Beatles' side B medley on *Abbey Road*
Choirs of loads to be borne into a future
As yet unforeseen but portending solitude
If not dolor, nights spent in dim precincts

Of the lost and dissolute. I desired dominion
Over the page, the apt phrase, a lyric mastery
That accuses. Instead, you chose nurturing
The ill and ill-disposed, tapping with your IV

The likeliest vein, carrying the red vial before
You obliviously like a candle in a sleepwalker's
Dream. Diastole and systole, you took pulses
In fingers both tapered and cool while I sought

The lineaments of gratified desire in a heart
More figurative than literal. Did you recall
As I do, how in fall 1970, there were mornings
We would meet in a snug café over cinnamon

Rolls and coffee or sip frosted mugs of pale
Lager on leaf-strewn afternoons? Under age
For such libations, we were never carded. I
Still conjure the shared embraces too few

And far between. Mid-December we embarked
On paths no longer coincident; you graduated
From the Tennessee Medical College in 1974,
And I published the title poem of my first book

In *Epoch* at Cornell University the next year.
Reading your obituary in the *Paducah Sun's*
Black columns in September 1995 was like
Stepping on a long thorn: it ripped the breath

Clean out of me. Your age was listed as 42,
But in fact, you were a year younger,
Although the surviving husband, the three
Children bereft of a mother rang dead true

As the knell of the First Christian Church
In Murray, Kentucky. A boy from the Delta,
I've grown old, a half-century of autumn leaves
Fallen between us like beaten gold, Teresa.

THE WAKING REVERIE

I stood on my back porch in the evening,
Alone. Like needlepoint, a few stars
Punched through the low-hanging clouds
And I listened to those big Canadian geese

Winging south, their long necks bent
To the migratory curve. I imagined you
Drifting beneath a satin counterpane,
How the brush before your darkened mirror

Crackled with enough static to lift this page
From your table of carved rosewood. In dreams
I walk those upstairs corridors twice fortunate,
Hoping to free your essence sealed in a bottle

Frosted green as absinthe. All poets partake
Of the harsh joy that attends solitude, but I
Conjure only you, reaching as I do for a ripe
Nectarine in my pocket, letting the juice trickle

Down my chin, the fruit not quite out of season
In this Delta suburb. In September, crickets
Still light up at moonrise, the toad's throat pulses
At the base of cracked masonry. But tonight,

Teresa, the wind whispers conspiracy in treetops,
And the gabbling flocks vanish along their flyway
Toward the Gulf. Plump droplets darken shingles
And I cross this threshold where all reverie ends.

THE WATCH

Four yellow roses, one for each month
In our brief season. In September, the lawns
Were still emerald, and at night the moon
Ran a shiver of dew through the grass.

The sun scatters fire-opals this morning,
And when the sexton turned his mower
One hundred-eighty degrees it spun out
A wreath at the foot of your blue-veined

Marble. But I remember that October most,
An owl hooded against the frost as it picked
The bones of careless mice, the scent of ripe
Persimmons in the frigid air. You are with me

Even now as you were then, your delicate
Shoulders shaken with laughter, redounding
From vacant carports and the scroll-worked
Eaves of houses we passed along lamplit streets

From Graceland to Paula. By November,
The red and gold leaves of sweetgum maples
Came spinning down like riddled biplanes
And pin oaks rained acorns on shingled roofs.

We would part in mid-December with no sequel;
You slipped the timepiece from your wrist,
Wordlessly handing it to me. For a quarter-
Century it ticked away with exquisite precision

Keeping the pulse of all the years from that one
To this. What do I have to give you now
But a few hours quiet watch on your lawn
And these fireflies' stone lanterns lighting up?

THE GHOSTLY HEART

Until one of us turned to unregenerate clay,
You vowed that you'd always love me.
My own people lie beneath the satin-lined
Rafters of the Odd Fellows cemetery

In Greenwood, Mississippi. The immortal
Robert Johnson was slipped a fatal dram
There in 1938, and Furry Lewis who could
Make his guitar fret like a bluebottle fly

Took his gift up to smoke-filled juke joints
In Memphis. One leg severed by a freight
Southbound on those twin ribbons of steel
That meet in infinity, he lived on the third

Floor of a flophouse when I first met him;
He'd play slide for hours with his pocket
Knife of dimpled bone, and we boys would
Listen spellbound by what we'd purchased

For a pint of Ten High whisky. In this Delta
Metropolis, only bluesman W. C. Handy,
Fingering the oily valves of his trumpet,
And Elvis arrested mid-swivel on Beale St.

Have been cast in bronze. Composers
And troubadours of a lesser stamp would
Be obliged to bide their time, hardly aware
That the genuine adept makes the era his

Or her own. I wanted to make your name
A byword for all things of beauty and grace,
Hoping to transcend those street-fights on
Overton Square, the evenings dealing Booray

In the backroom of nightclubs in Natchez.
Longing to win one kiss of salty eroticism
And celestial sweetness from your pert lips,
Teresa, I soon learned such things meant

Nothing unless freely given. I later marveled
How the four months of grace you lavished
On me couldn't be sounded on any keyboard
But were chords struck deep in a ghostly heart.

SOUND WISDOM

To venture that I was familiar with night
On the Delta, would be putting it all
Too mildly. In my late teens a pewter flask
Rode my hip and I tucked in my right boot

An eight-inch blade hafted in dimpled bone.
I didn't court trouble, but knew cemeteries
Were full of coffins, their rubber gaskets
Rotting in the August humidity. Every

Streetlamp smoked like a topaz in a box
Lined with grey felt. I'd conjure you
When I passed the country club
And heard the night watchman sifting

The static on his radio for the Cardinals
Double-header, soothing a quart of Bud,
The egg-salad sandwich and greasy chips
His wife bagged on the table beside him.

Unfamiliar footsteps would raise the hackles
On his Doberman's back, and he'd flick on
His battery-packed flashlight. But he would
Always make the padlock's tumblers ripple

And open up so I could take in a few innings
And talk about women. "Be sure to bide your
Your time, boy, but don't forget don't none 'em
Mind a man likin' it." He agreed that a nip

Now and then did no harm, "But get rid
Of that gut-fetcher; it's borrowin' trouble,
And she'll likely take you for a hood." He
Had one further admonition: "Death is kin to

A debt-collector; he just wants to get better
Acquainted—he don't necessarily want
To be friends." Perhaps to a genuine lady,
These words smack of chawbacon vulgarity,

But I for one number Walt among the ranks
Of the permanently wise. Decades have passed,
And you both rest beneath ledger-stones, names
Scored deeper than mallet and chisel can strike.

The Machinery of Night

While only a youth I visited the composing
Room of the Memphis *Commercial Appeal,*
Watched the green-hooded lamp illuminate
The old Linotype keyboard that my father's

Beautiful square hands plied so dexterously,
The slugs of hot lead dropping into slots,
The whole mechanism shifting and shuttling
Like a loom singing in Odysseus's great hall.

I had hoped our love would soon eclipse
The bales of printed pulpwood men bucked
Into truck beds below the icy loading dock
Then sped away beneath a blizzard of stars.

But I still remember the pumice-gritty soap
Black with carbon ink in the foaming dish
Above the lavatory sink when I rose for class,
The polyp-ridden snoring of a man who would

Not live to see twenty years of endless nightshifts
Go funneling down the drain into oblivion. I'd
Slide out the oaken bureau drawer, then open
With reverence his snibbed leather kit all

Aglitter with the cult tools of his thwarted calling,
The stemmed mouth mirror and wicked-hooked
Pick for probing the cusps of molars that otherwise
Twinkle like star sapphires. A scant sixteen months

Short of his DDS a perforated ulcer forced him
To withdraw from the University of Mississippi.
Meanwhile black columns in the Scripps-Howard
Rival *Press Scimitar* bruited about the summer

Evening soirees on your patio, fireflies lighting up
Switchboards of honeysuckle vine along the red
Brick wall, cool breezes winnowing your blue lawn.
I shunned the round of proms, cotillions, and dances,

Yet a certain sovereignty of spirit, as you called it,
Sounded in us a mutual chord, felt-cored hammers
Falling like 1970's autumn leaves, ghostly hands
Rummaging the banked ivories of the grand piano

On the Hotel Peabody's mezzanine. We met once
After your divorce, dining in their restaurant
On rack of lamb and a fine cabernet. Although
You took it as a matter of course, the sumptuous

Repast set me back a day's pay. Your pearls,
Teresa, took added luster from such radiant
Skin. When I bade you farewell, burly cicadas
High in elms were turning the machinery of night.

BACKWARD GLANCES

I. Woolgathering

I conceived of you as one who came and went
In many incarnations; others doubtless yielded
To imaginative excess: a striking blonde of 9th
Century Scandinavia, her cloak dyed purple
And pinned with golden disc brooches. She
Wore lightly enough a chatelaine gaudy with
Latchkeys of privilege and rank. But I put
Aside such chimeras before age fifteen. Still,
My own woolgathering persists like ground
Fog in the cotton field across the highway
Before the sun fires one opal in the dew. I
Recall a clarinet player who plied his trade
From Beale Street to Bourbon, dexterously
Fingering the keys, sounding out each note
Along reed, barrel, and bell as his instrument
Cooled down to a few bleak embers. He would
Then take his ease in some sequestered spot off
Stage, sipping a tall schooner of Schiltz. Did
He conjure a girl's fine-boned wrists, delicate
Shoulders, and muscular brown thighs, one
Who baffled his dreams even as he lovingly
Addressed his clarinet's baffle set after set,
Far into endless nights where waitresses moved
Through lounges bearing trays of gin-rickeys
That clink with ice? Better than most he knows
Those pawnshop windows smoking with gems
Wherein rosewood violins cure like hams, and scaly
Iridescent harmonicas bear mute witness to the fact
That blues without reedy wheezing and a little
Honest spit is neither fervent nor earnest. All this
In dream-light growing ever dimmer.

II. Dark Chambers

Perhaps your great-grandmother like my own
Would strike a match in the predawn dark;
Grafting the little hell-blossom to a lamp wick,
She'd adjust the englobed flame with the twist
Of a brass key. Once she was lovely as you,
Luxuriating in lavender bath crystals evenings
When the moon's burnished scythe crests high
Above a birch grove; the russet autumn leaves
Whisper like mowers' blades in wind-bent wheat.
Listen, Teresa, to the yellow braid and tassel
Percussing like rain on split-shingled roofs,
The long harvest rows at last fallen all one way.
But let's dismiss these rural idylls now quick only
In the minds of a select few. Return to the notion
Of metropolis from the Cyclopean stone of Mycenae
With its carved heraldic lions and beehive tombs
To the sun-struck glass and steel towers rising
From Manhattan to the Crescent City. It's New
Year's Eve in the Quarter and the ornate filigree
Of second-floor balustrades weeps like metal off
A soldering iron; the baroque scrollwork is crusted
Frosting on a wedding cake. It was a short
Stroll in sleeting rain to Elysian Fields, named
For Paris's *Champs-Élyseés*; after dinner you went
Up to our room, but I lingered at the bar, observing
How the publican poured Drambuie into a shot
Glass like some acolyte lighting a votive nub. I
Followed Prince Charles Edward's drink with two
Slings of Grand Marnier, and, the blue pilot light
In my brain turned low, I mounted the stairs to
Dark chambers where you still wait for all I know.

NARCISSUS TO THE MUSE

Lord, I did lay concern on myself lathering up
With mint-scented soap-on-a-rope, steam rising
From the tile floor, the spindrift suds sucked down
The swirling shower drain. I then drew aside

On tintinnabulating rings, the yellow curtain,
Groping for the means to towel off and slip on
My terry-cloth bathrobe. Sweat trickled down
The medicine cabinet mirror until my face

Rode up in the mercury-backed glass. I switched
On the Conair dryer, spellbound as my red-gold
Princeton haircut filled out in thick layers. No need
At fifteen for the Gillette platinum-edged blades,

I smeared English Leather like a heady balm
On my chest yet smooth as the tabula rasa.
It was for you, Teresa, that I put on the pleated
Oxford cloth shirt with the button-down collar,

Navy blue Levis and matching Gold Cup socks,
Then stepped into the oxblood penny loafers
With beef rolls. I shrugged on my wool cardigan
Still crackling with static this October morning

Over a half-century later in the year 2020.
Even before those days strolling HHS corridors
I remember turning the lighted dial of a radio
Surfing burbles and squeaks for the desired AM

Frequency breaking deep in the heart of the Delta.
I imagined Ty Cobb hearthside in the off-season,
The pine log sputtering and the resin seething out,
How he lovingly rubbed with oily porkchop bones

His bat of tight-grained maple to prevent chipping.
When its barrel connected, he could feel the tingling
Recoil in his palms and watch the horsehide pill's
Slow trajectory toward the rising tide in the bleachers.

When I toed the rubber in the junior-league,
The new-mown infield grass was more emerald
Than diamond. Every time I kicked and fired
I studied the physics of grip, pressure, and release,

The red stitching on the ball like a Homeric
Figure of eight shield. I was king of the hill,
And bided my time, handling the rosin-bag
Like a leather pouch bulging with gold-dust.

Unable to run my two-seam cutter over 88 m.p.h.,
I chipped at the strike-zone like a dark casement.
Batters would whiff too late a humming fastball
Turning into a wicked slider with my last-second

Flick of the wrist as the white spheroid rolled
Off my fingertips, and I bore the burden lightly
When sluggers swung, both knees buckling,
And muttering curses through the cured leaf,

Flung their helmets and returned to the dugout.
And don't forget the knuckle-ball rotating only once
In sixty and ½ feet around its cushion-cork center
Like a fisherman's cane pole and float hoping

The over-eager hitter would bite and go under.
I was aces too when it came to snagging
Line-drives hit back to the pitcher's mound,
My glove of Italian leather, web, palm, and heel,

Its lacing like the braid and tassel of harvest wheat,
The hinge kneaded dark with neat's foot oil,
Just the thing for hawking blue darters mid-air
And doubling-off some yokel headed for second.

Seldom did I hit a pitch beyond the infield,
But I could lay down a slow roller toward third
And round the bag in a spiked flurry before
The opposing catcher pounced and threw down,

Rifling the ball past the first baseman's mitt
Into right field. I stole home four times that season,
Loitering until some idiot lobbed the ball back
To his battery-mate without leaving his crouch

And I sprinted for the dish at a 4.32 clip,
Obliged to slide only once, the umpire's arms
Spread wide while the dust settled in titters
And the home crowd booed lustily all the while.

But by twelve I'd begun to envy upperclassmen
Punting pebble-grained pigskins in the bricky mid-
November air, those leather-sleeved jackets
Worn only by varsity stalwarts with the letter H

Sewn over their hearts, plus green chevrons
Like high-flying geese to signify captains.
A pastoral sport to be sure, and cheerleaders
Such as you with your blonde gypsy shag

Caught up in gymnastics and choreographed dance,
Brass tubas pumping out "Georgy Girl," to a flute's
Lilting stops. But our new football Americain
Made the push and pull of the rugby scrum tame,

Hardly the gut-thumping whump like a dozen
Umbrellas exploding along the scrimmage line.
If you listened you could hear shoulder pads pop
In the press box, the exchange of helmet paint

A smudge of pride in locker rooms from Whitehaven
To Bartlett. Then it was legal to chop-block,
Crack-back, horse-collar, and spear-tackling
Was the norm. It led to ruptured knee cartilage,

Torn ligaments, deep-thigh bruises, and concussed
Skulls. One September night under the lights
At Halle Stadium I rushed for 132 yards, my right
Thumb and ring finger fractured when linebackers

Put their Riddell helmets with multibar face masks
Through the ball I was coached to cradled in both arms.
Thus, the hammered gold band you reluctantly
Bestowed on him would never have fit me, Teresa.

Perhaps you still quicken that dark room silhouetted
Against a canvas screen pulled down like a shade where
Those 16 MM celluloid frames depict Viking exploits
Unfolding to the school projector's slow inexorable roll.

From the ruck and maul of our humanity, those piled limbs
Blown dead by a referee's whistle, we rise incorruptible,
Jumped up and come set again like a band of demons
Doomed to perpetual reenactment by reels run in reverse.

In those days long before overtime you'll not recall
How we went 6-2-2 that season, the team's collective
Fate held up as a warning to others by our taskmaster.
We bled in technicolor beneath those Friday night lights

And were consigned to a vault in black and white.
I came back three years later to watch from the track
You straying impassioned along the sidelines. Perhaps
Some disaffection akin to my own was even then moving

Through you like an unbidden joy. My hair cascaded
To my shoulders, my shirt opened at the throat. I wore
Brown corduroy bell-bottoms over brass-buckled boots.
I was drunk on apple wine and you looked at me so.

Two Parables

I often remember my father's people,
Their corner grocery on Rayburn St.
In south Memphis, the store's façade
Concrete, how the dead rust undulant
Siding painted aluminum cast a glare
Like water on the tiger lilies trembling
In the banked yard shored and buoyed up
By the beams of railroad ties. Cinders littered
The small lot and August nights bottles
Got busted, somebody cut. Emerald
Shards glittered malign as the fixed gaze
Of a stray cat. Dark lettering read: "Cold
Beer," "Snacks," "Soda," "No Loitering."
Among the heart-shaped catalpa leaves
Cicadas chattered like pressure cookers.
My grandfather behind his counter rang up
Variations deft as any metrical register,
Falstaff from the cooler, Dutch Masters
Panatelas, each empty box that I filled
With colorful lead soldiers an aromatic
Humidor. My sister would slip the bands
Of metallic foil on her fingers, seeking
The perfect fit. With a certain brawn
And swagger, the old man would
Stand to his round stump butcher's block,
Chopping blood sausage and liverwurst
Dubbed "goose liver" by his black customers.
But I loved Sundays when he closed up
At noon; somewhere a radio evangelist
Declaimed with a meetinghouse fervor,
And out back we'd rupture the casks
Of watermelon sunk in a washtub chock
Full of ice. I'd spit out the seeds embedded
In the red fruit, black index notches
Of the *Oxford English Dictionary;*

Even then the word-hoard seemed
Ripe for plunder. My lovely mother
During her earliest years resembled you.
Each morning she'd court the calliope
Hummingbird with its purple throat.
It siphoned nectar from a honeysuckle's
Tiny floral Victrola, its choral wheedling
A blur amid bee balm and sage. The male
Weighs less than the star of a penny
Bright with rheum. The female constructs
Her nest out of a spider's spun gossamer.
Reared in a house on Grand Boulevard
In Greenwood, Mississippi, my maternal
Grandfather primed his rage with bonded
Whisky. He loved to roll the bones, to shoot
The jive with dock-hands behind the Quinn
Drug Co. A blue .38 riding his hip, he passed
The collection plate odd Sundays, blackjack
Tucked in his breast pocket. Some devout
Church-goers whispered how a white hood
And sheet haunted his bedroom closet.
Oblivious to such rumors my mother
Went serenely about her daily rounds,
Sun cresting the hemlocks, mist burning
Off the lawn in fiery opalescent tints.

NIGHTHAWKS

I. The Rayburn Street Grocery

My grandfather's broad leather strap
Served to strop his straight-edge razor
And polish my butt when I got out-of-line.
He broke the night-long fast with biscuits
Thick as his gold pocket watch, sourdough
Gravy and blood sausage. Lean, blinking
Behind wire-rimmed spectacles, one regular
Customer in the old man's shop swore he
Ate so much "It made him po' to carry it."
During high school he was state champion
In Mississippi's high-jump, then spent
Five years as a relief-pitcher for St. Louis
While they were still called the Browns.
His later years were cast in sepia tones.
In his broad-band fedora he resembled
A slumped figure in Edward Hopper's
Nighthawks, the stark oil on canvas
Depiction of film noire figures in a diner,
Napkin dispensers on the counter, coffee
Tanks in the background, porcelain mugs
Awaiting glazed sinkers our generation
Dubbed doughnuts. Hopper's brooding
Composition requires no "voice over"
Or the various subtitles I rehearse here.

II. The Brister Tower Library

Clerks in the University of Memphis library,
Richard Crowson and I would engage daily
In verbal badinage. Even before sketching
His name into the pages of the *Jackson Sun*
And the *Wichita Eagle*, he remarked to me
With a smart drollery how his "poetry phase"

Had ended at eighteen. My rejoinder
Delineated the boredom of drawing "Heckle
And Jeckle" on deckle-edged butcher paper
From my grandfather's meat locker before
I turned six. Still, I peered in when old
"Ricky the Crow" opened his musty text
To Dürer's *Knight, Death, and the Devil,*
And he'd listen to me recite "Byzantium"
By the restless warden of Thoor Ballylee.

III. The Daily Round

My father's mother baked cornbread
Apportioned in thick-sliced wedges;
Ringing up purchases on the register
While my grandfather napped, she'd
Daub at various pigments come evening.
Although she never finished high school,
A certain fluency guided the sure dip
And glide of her bristled horsehair brush
As a red barnlike timber-truss bridge
Spanning a blue stream would converge
On plain cotton smelling of linseed oil.
Once an art dealer chanced on the store,
But she claimed her paintings were too
Poor to sell and too dear to give away.
Her genuine avocation was the canning
Of blackberry preserves: "bramble jam"
As the neighbors would have it. My own
Mother, who measured out her girlhood
With a sterling silver sugar shell,
Declared it talent squandered on a man
Whose sole concern was the daily round.
Resettling the dent in his hat, the old gent
Would shrug on his grey trench coat and
Vanish into October's early morning fog.

Another Realm of Discourse

I. My Father's Household

As a youth, my father devoured flannel
Cakes mauled in blackstrap molasses, an
Electric percolator's cover knob rattling
Like a lone brown penny spun heads up
On a wooden counter. His grandmother
Dipped snuff, and the repurposed blue
Maxwell House can chimed like a barber
Shop cuspidor. Buttered potatoes sweeter
Than the notes of an ocarina graced most
Depression-era supper tables. Piping hot,
A yam often bore the mark of the spade
In its orange skin. Soon my father's pores
Squinted like accordion beads beneath
The blazing sun at Peleliu and Tarawa.
I still own the bolt-action rifle he took off
A Japanese Imperial Marine he killed
In the heat-refracted nightmare of single
Combat. An amphibious soldier's only
Respite lay in cracking open a cold quart
Of Falstaff. The amber bottle's lip fumed
As he slaked in humidity for all the world
Akin to the Mississippi Delta in August.

II. My Mother's Schooling

You are always first to enter my mind
Every time I recall my mother's text on
Etiquette purchased at Mississippi State
College for Women. Never mind the house
Wine, be it crackling Italian red intended
To accompany bread and Brie or an ice-
Hot chardonnay served by the carafe.
She told me to observe the cork's brand,

Its frail hermetic scrimshaw, whenever
Sommelier or steward broaches a bottle,
And always to sniff for any hint of taint.
Neither gourmand nor tosspot, I noted
Scrupulously each wine glass: base,
Stem, bowl, and rim. I often longed
To trace the ruby, amber-lit claret's
Translucence to its roots in the Latin
Claritas or a vineyard's cultivated rows.
Like you, I preferred the sacraments
Of sun and soil, eschewing the impulse
To filter these through the high artifice
Of institutional adornment such as light
Staining the windows of Sainte Chapelle.

III. Coda

Our own generation endowed the locution
"Plastic" with a negative resonance. We did
Not recall that it derives from the Greek: *plassein*
"To shape or mold." How many lyrics spun
Out of 33 rpm discs awakened in us strains
Haunting as The Beatles' "Long and Winding
Road," the molten gold and plangent loveliness
Of Elvis' "It's Now or Never"? Can we forget
Gladys Knight's rendering of "Midnight Train
To Georgia" penned by Ole Miss quarterback
Jim Weatherly? Teresa, the wine list was least
On my mind seated opposite you one last time
That rain-swept evening in April. Moistening
Your lower lip, you knew I couldn't forgo a taste.

WAVELENGTHS

I. Predawn Quest

Before dawn colors the horizon I awake,
Watching stars congeal to signs any soul
Might deem auspicious; regarding starry
Leaves of sweetgum maples, their cork stems
Sealed by barbed frost setting the landscape
Ablaze with rich autumnal hues, I even now
Evoke the whitewashed "cracker box" house
On South Prescott and its upright radio:
Electric sap seemed to burble and squeak
As I turned the knob searching for precisely
The right frequency on our antique Philco,
Its art deco cabinet resembling New York's
Chrysler building, swank lobby adorned
With amber, onyx, and marble. I shunned
The big band orchestral strains, Teresa,
For Cannonball Adderly's barreling sax,
All the hungry rock and roll artists cutting
Sides on the Sun and Stax labels right here
In Memphis. Elvis Presley, Little Richard,
And Jerry Lee Lewis, plugged into juke boxes
Of neon red, blue, and gold, were quaking
Ramshackle barbeque dives from Beale St.
To Old Highway 51. One October afternoon
At my grandparents' Rayburn Street Grocery
Afforded ample 90 proof how hard it was for
The other side to "get over," a poor neighbor-
Hood where feckless men with no intention
Of paying midwives who birthed their brood
Were often branded with the opprobrium,
"Granny-Dogger." Yet the specter of Elvis
Sporting the piped braid of a Loew's State
Usher, another "Humes High greaser" who
Would graduate to downshifting his Crown

Electric two-door on slow grades between
Tupelo and Nashville, inspired every Delta
Lyricist to pursue those reflecting lines zipping
By like tracer bullets on darkened highways.

II. Legacies of Loss

Always it seems I return to the River City's
Once and future "King," his hair pomaded
With rose oil and Vaseline, Ace comb tracks
Shining like outsized record grooves. My folks
Would let me stay all night on Rayburn St.
While they watched Elvis play the Overton
Park Shell in the evenings; those early gigs
Accreted like pearls Col. Tom Parker lovingly
Cultivated while groundskeepers mopped
Urine gushed in the aisles by enraptured
Teenage girls. Presley would work the ache
Of a fretted six-string into callused fingers
Crooning "Love Me Tender," before he broke
Into hip-gyrating rhythms, and the soulful
Wail of "Jailhouse Rock." It was a full decade
Before another King would be coolly dialed up
Into a rifle scope's crosshairs and nailed while
Leaning on the Lorrainne Motel's second-floor
Railing. I little realized then we had inherited
A legacy of loss greater than we could dream.

III. The Reckoning

You and I grew to maturity while the lads
From Liverpool were at floodtide. The Beatles
Disbanded by the time we paired off, their mantra
Of love not lost on us. Our day-to-day assignations
Were curiously nocturnal but didn't preclude
The dawn rendezvous when everything seems
Birth-wet and new and delight resides in pure

Anticipation. But didn't George Harrison insist
"All Things Must Pass" and you knew it must
Be so well before I did; our first parting occurred
In a small café the morning of December 14, 1970.
Somewhere I'm still sifting that old radio dial
In the predawn dark pricked out with stars
For some wavelength bearing me home to you.

Elusive Couplings

I. Grand Boulevard

My earliest memories have taproots deep
In Greenwood, Mississippi's lush Delta soil,
My mother's hometown where barns burst
With cotton ginned and carded in the year
Of my birth, 1951. Named for the Choctaw's
Last great chieftain, Leflore County's small
Abode teemed with buyers dealing in the cash
Crop, stud poker, bonded whisky, and onyx-
Eyed lovelies in the bustling red-light district
South of the Yazoo River bridge. Engineers
Guiding the Columbus and Greenville line
Diesels tugged on their brass-mounted horns
And waved to me; but I dreamed of old coal-
Burning locomotives freighting picked bolls
To all points of the compass, smoke batting
Their tall stacks. I often imagined fabulous
Throttlemen tapping at valves and meters,
Wrenches clinking, even as I tinker with
This faltering metric. Perhaps years later,
A weary girl fitfully sleeping beneath silk
Sheets, you sensed a train's slow passing
By the tremor in cabinets filled with amethyst
And crystal. Then it seemed chuffing iron
Horses traveled more on wine glasses than
Steel rails burnished smooth by gliding tons.

II. Rayburn Street

My father's parents opened the Rayburn St.
Corner grocery in Memphis five years later;
Derelict crossties shored the side yard's steep
Embankment heaped with cinders. Shards
Of broken beer bottles shone like bright topaz
Scattered in some slag heap. Railroad tracks

Ran a quarter-mile to the south and grandma
Would fix lunch for hoboes—thick pork chops
And french fries—who knocked at her kitchen
Door. They would often chalk an angel curbside
As a signal to fellow bindlestiffs. A retired switch-
Man, Mr. Linten would lean on the red cooler
August nights and swig a chill quart of Falstaff.
Seersucker cap pushed back on his forehead,
He'd take his pocket watch from its trickling
Gold chain and let me examine it for hours.
Consumption carried him off one day
Holding fast to my grandfather's hand. Once
I'd seen the change of ten summers I flattened
Minted coppers under the grinding wheels
Of the Illinois Central, but the black youths
I sorted with called me a fool because a penny
Redeemed two crème filled cookies in the store.
I little understood the bleak necessities of want
Or those small pleasures that must attend them.

III. Our Own Couplings

No station or roundhouse came with the Lionel
Train set circa. 1961 I got for Christmas several
Months before. But I hearkened to the clack
Of what dawned on me were mattress springs
Bearing my parents away in the bedroom next
My own when I was an infant. Red lanterns
Swinging from the caboose receded as I drifted
Into slumber. Not a soul listened for our own
Lovemaking's low commotion decades later.
Teresa, we dined on chicken cordon bleu
In the evening and popped the cork on a bottle
Of excellent chardonnay before climbing stairs
To find our mutual appetites merely whetted
For elusive couplings forever about to connect.

TERESA: THE INTERLUDE

Perhaps it was your love for the things
Of this world that beguiled me,
When you delicately turned in first light
A bronze beetle's lacquered carapace,

Or fingered the carnal whorl of a rose
Climbing the garden trellis, its fleshy
Petals trembling with dew. How often
You'd marvel at a snail negotiating

Bark chips with exquisite twin antennae,
Its pewter track and scrolled shell like
A violin's sorrowings. I little knew then
It was Lorca's *duende* that lit your eyes

Of cerulean blue or the brief span left me
To stand in their radiance. After we parted,
I'd watch beneath my ledge a magnolia leaf
Each new day from the prevailing darkness.

Yet we met a decade later in New Orleans,
Youth's luster still rounding your cheeks,
The chandeliers spilling crystal and nickel
Throughout Le Pavillon's palatial corridors.

We would conspire over gin cocktails, no
Bitters, triple olives spit on one toothpick.
Mornings you'd wear my pinstripe shirt
At our room-service breakfast, black coffee

And Belgian waffles wobbling in cascades
Of maple syrup, the trees tapped in April
When the sap rises, the sugary confection
Distilled and stoppered in golden phials.

Quintessential loveliness but seldom cloys
The palate, and come noon we'd stroll
Bourbon Street, listening to a harmonica's
Reedy wheezing, an old bootblack's rag

Snap like .32-caliber shot, his patrons
Enthroned and brass foot-rests locked
Into place. You adored the decorative
Wrought iron balustrades in the Quarter

When it was too early for saxophones
Squiggling blues or clarinets cooling
Down to a few bleak embers at the end
Of evening sets in La Belle Esplanade.

The Riverwalk brought us full circle,
Tugs, tankers, and barges churning
The Mississippi mid-channel, the current
Meandering drunkenly toward the Gulf.

Suddenly we stood once more on the bluff
Above Memphis, our youth summed up
In the plangent hooting of raptors
Making wing for Mud Island after dusk.

TERESA: NIGHTS ON THE DELTA

I. Side A

I can still summon up those summer nights
On the Delta, when my antique Underwood's
Basket shift clicked like a fisherman's bait box
Teeming with live crickets. I'd align a sheet
Of rice paper in the platen and roll it into place
Deftly as my mother putting her white pinafores
Through a wringer before pinning a hamperful
To the clothesline. Emerald fireflies were rising
And falling like rootless stars while I composed
At the trestle board table, frosted mug beside me
Brimming golden Schiltz that I lovingly soothed
Into the wee hours during July of my twentieth
Year. You were my motive and cue for passion
Even then; I'd lift cold iron doors of red
And blue mailboxes bolted down curbside, posting
A sheaf of poems meant to evoke the comeliness
Of your speech and its liquid sonorities. A manila
Envelope returned one poem lighter from *Steelhead*,
Edited by Louis Jenkins in Duluth, Minnesota, almost
It seemed before the evening's chill dews and damps
Had dried on my palm. Elated, I felt launched in
Earnest, but now I brood over your ledger-stone
In the Murray City Cemetery where granite heaves
At its own glittering mass like the sea. The sexton
Wears on his belt a ring of keys like a woman's hand-
Bones. To him sadness is a watermelon's heart
Salted down, good whisky poured over the grave
Of a beautiful stranger. Shouldering a spade, he
Wipes sweat from his neck with a kerchief dyed
Midnight blue. He pauses. At his ear, patient
As needlepoint, the gnat's psalm.

II. Side B

October moon ripens colder than a honeydew melon
On the hill's shoulder. Scattered flocks begin to gather,
Grackles playing the raucous bones of autumn. When
Oil tins banged in our storage room my father described
Depression-era migrants, how a hobo in tattered flannel
Would stoke a furnace till dark to buy a side of bacon,
Then fry spattering pork on his blunt-edged shovel.
Meanwhile, my mother's people dined on sumptuous
Steaks or roasts while a bottle of Grand Marnier
Waited on the teak sideboard to be poured over
Dollops of vanilla ice-cream for dessert. The distance
Between their manor house on Greenwood's boulevard
And the shotgun shanty where Dad dwelled as a boy
Seemed wider than Keesler Bridge spanning the Yazoo
River meandering drunkenly south toward Vicksburg.
Now each dawn I part my beige burlap drapes
To sun so abundant it's like slashing a sack of grain.
Genteel poverty has been the wage of lending amplitude
To the protein heat our bodies sowed on satin sheets
So many decades ago. Even now you are with me
In all seasons: when I watch a cedar waxwing chip
At iced rowanberries with its beak or perhaps pause
As a locust splits and crawls out of its larval blister
Into song. I dial up the Beatles' "Long and Winding
Road" on a radio crackling with static and conjure
Those dusk to dawn interludes sleeping side by side,
The spectral celestial choir McCartney deplored
Bearing us to other shores, one banked in the temporal
World, the other in eternity. For me, those vinyl-tracked
Lyrics had more to do with a potter's wheel—"Truth is
Beauty, / beauty, truth"—than some forgotten DJ's
Turntable. Draw the curtain, Teresa.

THE FULL RECKONING

I. The Quickening

A master cabinet-maker augured concentric,
Sweet-scented roses from rosewood, and fitted
Dowel pins into the resin-embalmed boards
Of your hand-carved wardrobe. He shaped
The cabinet doors like ornate seraph wings,
Each opening on the burnished satin gowns
You'd step into with winsome aplomb a few
Years beyond puberty. Then your radiant
Skin would bear only the scar of a smallpox
Vaccination pricked out with a needle before
Seething pustular eruptions were banished
From our midst. Four centuries previous
To our own the immortal Bard of the Avon
Decried a similar affliction visited on him
By his beguiling "dark mistress." Teresa,
The nocturnal meetings we shared savored
More of fleshly covenant than assignation
During autumn, 1970, when rain knocked
Russet leaves and skull-capped acorns off
Pin oak boughs spanning Overton Park.

II. The Southwest Twin

Again, I recall how silken-bearded angels glared
Back at me wandering the rows of harvest corn,
A blue-denimed lad agog at ripening maize rooted
In fertile Delta soil; I often flailed at circling crows,
Their beaks intent on tallying the yellow abacus
Of each unshucked ear. Sometimes I'd stumble
Onto red-jacketed and brass-gleaming shotgun
Shells ejected by irate farmers minding their own
Crops with lead pellets rather than gravel pecked
From loam. A decade later we'd fall into

The muffled drumming of a motorcade headed
For the drive-in theater, twin screens flickering
Like heat-lighting along the skyline. Headlamps
Were dimmed and tickets punched beneath stars
Peppering the cobalt firmament. We'd indulge
In the barbaric splendor of Bacardi-laced Coke
And the opulent fleur-de-lis locked in each kernel
Of popcorn. For you, it amounted to a diversion,
You, who'd never once seen a carpenter cancel
His pay with dull lead wetted on his tongue's tip.

III. Murray, Kentucky: 2022

I remember the mist-shrouded October
Evening when I first glimpsed in your laughter
The simple pathos of a moment that rendered
The future irrevocable as the past. But tonight
An ark hoarding your ivory-petaled bones shines
Like a long drawer of exquisite relics. Red roses
Sent to your emerald-sodded plot stand opposite
Your wedded name sand-blasted into granite.
I never enclose a card, not wishing to trespass
On another's sense of propriety. Somehow,
I could never countenance the notion of being
Loved by anyone but you. Even now I conjure
Oceans of red wheat like the slow roll of a lion's
Shoulder. Turn this page in its own light.

ACKNOWLEDGMENTS

Grateful acknowledgment is extended to the editors of the following journals and anthologies, in which these poems first appeared, some in slightly different versions.

Arkansas, Arkansas: Writings and Writers from the Delta to the Ozarks: "Warm Latitudes"; "The Death of Georg Trakl (1887-1914)"; "A Last Word"; "James Bowie: Bexar, 1836"

The Arkansas Review: "Sleeping Over on Highway 78"; "The Watch"; "Nighthawks"; "Wavelengths"; "The Ghostly Heart"; "Sound Wisdom"; "The Machinery of Night"

The Ark River Review: "A Last Word"

The Denver Quarterly: "A Blues Funeral Mood"

Epoch: "The Scarecrow"

The Georgia Review: "The Years Between"; "The Waking Reverie"

The Gettysburg Review: "Piano Player"; "James Bowie, Bexar: 1836"; "Travis"; "The Fruits of Victory"; "Alamo Pyre: March 6, 1836"; "San Antonio de Bexar"; "Kentucky Long Rifles"; "Bonham on the Night Prairie"; "The Visitation"; "Backward Glances"

The Good People of Gomorrah: "Forecast"; "The Glassblower"

The Kenyon Review: "Kentucky Gunsmith: Long Rifle, 1833"; "Berserker"

Madrona: "Walk in the Cemetery at Dawn"

Raccoon: "Ghost of the Coal Miner"; "To Rafael Alberti"; "Turning the Corner for Home"; "Litany of Rain"

The Sewanee Review: "Degüello"; "The Militia Shirt"; "Gregorio Ezparza"; "Santa Anna's Spurs"; "Aftermath: Dusk at the Alamo"; "The Natchez Sandar Fight"; "Expiation"; "Farewell"

Shenandoah: "Crockett"; "Crockett by Firelight"

The Southern Poetry Review: "Drawing A Sea-Horse"; "The Death of Georg Trakl (1887-1914)"

Steelhead: "The Tree House"

Tar River Poetry: "Lizard"
Ten Poets: "*Degüello*"
West Branch: "Eric Von Schmidt: Beyond Canvas"
The Xavier Review: "Teresa: Nights on the Delta"
Yarrow: "Angler"; "Revel"; "The Priest and the Toad"

ABOUT THE AUTHOR

FLOYD COLLINS received his baccalaureate degree in English from the University of Memphis. He earned an MFA in Creative Writing and a PhD in Twentieth Century American and British Literature at the University of Arkansas. His previous collections include *Seamus Heaney: The Crisis of Identity*, *What Harvest: Poems on the Siege and Battle of the Alamo*, and *My Back Pages: The Teresa Poems*. His poetry has appeared in a number of anthologies, including *Arkansas, Arkansas: Writers* and *Writings from the Delta to the Ozarks*. He has served on the faculty of the University of Arkansas, Quincy University, and Gordon State College. During the 2000-2001 academic year he was Shakespeare Seminar Scholar and Poet-in-Residence at Wabash College. His poetry and critical essays appear regularly in *The Arkansas Review*, *The Georgia Review*, *The Gettysburg Review*, *The Kenyon Review*, *Literary Matters*, and *The Sewanee Review*. Collins was awarded the Allen Tate Prize in 2007. He was born in Charleston, South Carolina and currently resides in Fayetteville, Arkansas.